MW01135191

FROM ZERO TO BROKER HERO

HOW TO BECOME A COMMERCIAL LOAN BROKER

WITHOUT A DEGREE.

COPYRIGHT

DISCLAIMER

The information contained in this book is for general information purposes only. The author and publisher have made every effort to ensure the accuracy and completeness of the information provided. However, they make no guarantees, warranties, or representations, express or implied, concerning the information's accuracy, reliability, or completeness.

This book is not intended as a substitute for professional advice. The author and publisher shall not be held liable for any loss or damage, including but not limited to incidental or consequential damages, arising from the use of, or reliance upon, any information provided in this book.

The reader is advised to consult with an appropriate professional before making any decisions or taking any actions based on the information contained in this book.

The reader is also responsible for complying with all applicable laws and regulations, including licensing requirements, when implementing any of the strategies or ideas presented in this book.

DEDICATION

This book is dedicated to all aspiring entrepreneurs who seek success in the commercial loan brokerage industry without a formal degree. Your determination, persistence, and hard work are the driving forces that will lead you to achieve your goals and dreams. I also dedicate this book to my family, friends, and mentors who have supported and inspired me throughout my journey in commercial lending.

TABLE OF CONTENTS

INTRODUCTION

The commercial loan industry can be a lucrative and rewarding career for those interested in finance and passionate about helping businesses grow. As a commercial loan broker, you can play a critical role in connecting businesses withthe financing they need to achieve their goals and grow their operations.

But becoming a successful commercial loan broker requires more than just an interest in finance. It requires a combination of skills, knowledge, and strategy. This book is designed to provide aspiring commercial loan brokers with the information they need to get started in the industry and build a successful career.

Throughout the pages of this book, you will learn the basics of commercial loan brokering, including the skills and education needed to succeed, the different types of loans and financing options available, and how to market and promote your services to potential clients.

You will also gain insights from experienced commercial loan brokers, who will share their strategies for success, including tips for building a strong network, providing excellent customer service, and staying up to date with industry trends and regulations.

Whether you are new to the industry or have some experience as a loan broker, this book will provide you with the tools and knowledge you need to take your career to the next level and become a successful commercial loan broker.

Whether you're tired of working at a dead-end job, your company is facing layoffs, or you just want to be your own boss, the opportunity to become a loan broker might be a perfect fit. This book gives you an in-depth look at how to become a loan broker, how to start a loan broker business, how to make money in the world of commercial capital, and how to be a commercial loan broker that is recognized and trusted in the industry:

CHAPTER 1

UNDERSTANDING THE COMMERCIAL LOAN BROKER INDUSTRY

WHAT IS A COMMERCIAL LOAN BROKER?

A commercial loan broker is a professional who specializes in helping businesses secure financing for their operations. They work with various lenders, including banks, credit unions, and private lenders, to find the best loan options for their clients.

Commercial loan brokers can assist with a variety of loan types, including commercial mortgages, working capital loans, equipment financing, and lines of credit. They can help businesses with financing needs, such as purchasing new equipment, expanding their operations, or consolidating debt.

Commercial loan brokers will assess the business's financial needs and creditworthiness to find the best loan options for their clients. They will then work with lenders to negotiate loan terms and find the best interest rates and repayment schedules for their clients.

Commercial loan brokers play an important role in helping businesses secure financing that may be otherwise difficult to obtain. They can provide businesses with access to a broader range of loan options and can help simplify the loan application and approval process. Additionally, working with a commercial loan broker can save businesses time and money by helping them find the best loan options more quickly and with lower interest rates.

THE DIFFERENT TYPES OF BUSINESS LOAN BROKERS

There are various commercial loan brokers, each specializing in a specific form of commercial loan. Here are some examples:

This sort of commercial loan broker specializes in providing small businesses with loans. They typically collaborate with lenders who provide Small Business Administration (SBA) loans, equipment financing, and other small business loans.

This sort of commercial loan broker specializes in providing loans for the acquisition and refinancing of commercial real estate. They collaborate with financiers who provide commercial mortgages, bridge, construction, and other commercial real estate loans.

This sort of commercial loan broker specializes in providing financing for the acquisition of equipment. They collaborate with lenders who provide equipment leasing, equipment loans, and other forms of equipment purchase financing.

This form of commercial loan broker is specialized in providing businesses with merchant cash advances. A merchant cash advance is a form of financing in which a business obtains cash in advance and repays the advance with a percentage of future sales.

This sort of commercial loan broker specializes in securing funding for international trade transactions. They collaborate with financiers who provide import-export financing, letters of credit, and other forms of international trade financing.

This sort of commercial loan broker specializes in providing businesses with factoring services. In a factoring transaction, a company sells its accounts receivable to a third party at a discount in exchange for immediate cash.

Based on their experience, knowledge, and interests, commercial loan brokers specialize in various categories of commercial loans. By specializing in a particular form of commercial loan, they are able to offer guidance and expertise to clients seeking financing in that area.

WHAT ARE THE BENEFITS OF BECOMING A LOAN BROKER?

There are several benefits of becoming a loan broker, including:

Flexibility: As a loan broker, you have the flexibility to work for yourself or with a company. You can set your own schedule and work from home or an office.

High earning potential: Loan brokers can earn a significant income through commissions and fees for successfully securing loans for their clients. Your income potential will depend on your experience, skills, and the types of loans you specialize in.

Opportunities for growth: The lending industry is constantly changing, providing opportunities for growth and learning. As a loan broker, you can continually expand your knowledge and expertise in the field.

Helping clients achieve their financial goals: Loan brokers play a vital role in helping clients secure financing for their businesses or personal needs. You can help clients achieve their goals and contribute to their financial success.

Building a network: Loan brokers work with lenders, real estate agents, and other professionals in the finance industry. This provides opportunities to build a professional network that can benefit your career and business.

Contributing to the economy: By helping businesses secure financing, loan brokers contribute to the growth of the economy. This can be a rewarding experience, knowing that you are helping to make a positive impact in your community.

Low start-up costs: Compared to other businesses, starting a loan brokerage requires relatively low start-up costs. You can work from home or rent a small office, and you don't need expensive equipment to get started.

Diverse client base: Loan brokers work with a diverse range of clients, including individuals, small businesses, and large corporations. This can provide opportunities to work on different types of loans and gain experience with various industries.

Entrepreneurial opportunity: As a loan broker, you can start your own business and become an entrepreneur. You have the opportunity to build your own brand and business model, providing a sense of independence and control over your career.

Intellectual challenge: Securing financing for clients can be a challenging and intellectually stimulating process. It requires analyzing financial statements, understanding creditworthiness, and negotiating loan terms, among other skills.

Personal satisfaction: As a loan broker, you have the opportunity to make a positive impact on your clients' lives. By helping them secure financing, you can help them achieve their goals and improve their financial situation.

In summary, becoming a loan broker offers a variety of benefits, including flexibility, high earning potential, growth opportunities, diverse client base, low start-up costs, entrepreneurial opportunity, intellectual challenge, personal satisfaction, and contribution to the economy.

HOW CAN A COMMERCIAL LOAN BROKER DEVELOP THEIR NETWORK?

A commercial loan broker can develop a network in a variety of ways, such as:

Attend Industry Events Attending industry events such as conferences, seminars, and networking events is a fantastic way to meet new people and expand your network. These events are typically attended by other industry professionals, such as financiers, investors, and loan brokers.

Join Professional Associations: Joining professional associations, such as the National Association of Commercial Loan Brokers (NACLB) and the Commercial Finance Association (CFA), can help you network with other industry professionals. These associations frequently host networking events, conferences, and online forums that can be utilized to expand your professional network.

Utilize Social Media: Social media platforms such as LinkedIn are an excellent method to network with other industry professionals. You can search for and connect with other loan brokers, lenders, and investors using LinkedIn. Additionally, you can join industry-specific LinkedIn groups and partake in discussions to build your reputation and network.

Providing value to your clients is the first step in constructing a solid network. You can provide value to your clients as a commercial loan broker by providing them with resources, advice, and connections to other industry professionals. By serving as a valuable resource for your clients, you can develop their trust and credibility, which can result in referrals and new business.

Reach Out to Potential Referral Partners: Identify potential referral partners who work with business proprietors and entrepreneurs, such as real estate agents, attorneys, and accountants. Reach out to these professionals and suggest collaborating on deals or exchanging client referrals. By establishing solid relationships with referral partners, you can expand your network and acquire new clients.

HOW CAN A COMMERCIAL LOAN INTERMEDIARY ACQUIRE CUSTOMERS?

A commercial loan broker can acquire customers via the following methods:

Referrals are one of the most effective methods for a commercial loan broker to acquire clients. You can solicit referrals from both your current clients and other industry professionals, such as real estate agents, attorneys, and accountants.

Marketing: Creating a marketing strategy can be an effective method for attracting new customers. You can reach potential customers through a variety of marketing channels, including social media, email marketing, and paid advertising.

Building a robust network of industry professionals can also help you acquire clients. Attend industry events, join professional organizations, and utilize social media to network with potential clients and referral sources.

By providing value to prospective clients, you can establish yourself as a reliable advisor and increase your chances of acquiring new business. Offer potential clients free whitepapers, webinars, and educational content to demonstrate your expertise and provide value.

Establish a Strong Online Presence: In today's digital era, it is essential to have a strong online presence. Create a professional website highlighting your services and expertise, and optimize it for search engines so potential clients can easily find you.

Specialize in a Niche: By specializing in a particular niche or industry, you can distinguish yourself from other commercial loan brokers and attract clients who are seeking expertise in that area.

Remember that it requires time and effort to build a successful commercial loan brokerage business. You can attract new customers and develop a successful business by employing a variety of strategies and consistently providing value to your clients.

HOW DOES A COMMERCIAL LOAN ADVISER EARN MONEY?

A commercial loan counselor can earn money through commissions or fees associated with loan transactions. The amount of money a commercial loan broker can earn depends on the type of loan, its size, and the commission or fee structure.

Here are some common methods by which commercial loan advisers generate income:

Transactions based on commission are the most common method for commercial loan brokers to generate income. The broker earns a commission, which is typically a percentage of the loan amount when a loan is approved and funded.

Some commercial loan facilitators charge up-front fees to cover the cost of their services, which may include loan packaging, underwriting, and due diligence. Typically, these fees are non-refundable and may be a fixed rate or a proportion of the loan amount.

In addition to commissions and up-front fees, some commercial loan brokers charge processing fees to cover the costs associated with processing loan applications. These fees are typically paid by the borrower as a fixed rate.

Points: Points are loan origination fees levied by lenders. B Commercial loan brokers can earn a portion of these points by introducing the borrower to the lender Points are typically expressed as a proportion of the loan amount.

It is essential for commercial loan brokers to disclose their commission and fee structures to their clients. Brokers must also comply with all laws and regulations governing their industry, such as those governing disclosure and equitable lending practices.

THE FUTURE OF BUSINESS FINANCING BROKERING

Several trends and developments are likely to shape the future of commercial loan brokerage, including:

As technology continues to advance, commercial loan brokerage will likely become increasingly automated. For instance, AI and machine learning could be utilized to automate underwriting and due diligence.

Greater Emphasis on Relationships: Despite the possibility of automation, relationships are likely to continue to play a crucial role in commercial loan brokerage. Developing solid relationships with customers, referral partners, and lenders will continue to be crucial to achieving success.

Focus on Niche Specialization: As industry competition continues to intensify, commercial loan brokers may choose to differentiate themselves by focusing on niche specialization. This may involve specializing in specific loan categories, industries, or geographic regions.

As businesses become more complex and diverse, it is likely that commercial loan structures will also become more complex. This will necessitate that commercial loan broker have a comprehensive comprehension of the available loan types and loan structures.

Greater Regulatory Oversight: In the coming years, the commercial loan brokerage industry will likely encounter increased regulatory scrutiny as regulators focus on protecting consumers and ensuring fair lending practices. This will necessitate that commercial loan counselor remain current on regulatory requirements and best practices for compliance.

In general, technology, specialization, relationships, and regulatory compliance are likely to influence the future of commercial loan brokerage. In the coming years, commercial loan brokers who can acclimate to these trends and developments will likely be successful.

From zero to broker hero

CHAPTER 2

THE DIFFERENT WAYS TO BECOME A COMMERCIAL LOAN BROKER

While a degree is not always required, having a background in finance or business can be helpful in gaining the necessary knowledge and skills for the job. Many loan brokers receive on-the-job training through internships or entry-level positions in the financial industry. Some employers also offer training programs for new loan brokers.

While certification is not always required, some loan brokers choose to become certified through organizations such as the National Association of Mortgage Brokers or the American Institute of Certified Public Accountants.

Gaining experience in the financial industry is important for becoming a successful loan broker. This may include working in underwriting, credit analysis, or loan processing.

By following these steps and continuously improving your skills and knowledge, you can become a successful loan broker and build a rewarding career in the financial industry.

HIGHLIGHT

Build your network: Loan brokers often rely on networking to build relationships with lenders and clients. Attend industry events, join professional organizations, and build a strong online presence to establish your reputation.

Gain relevant education and experience: While formal education is not a requirement for becoming a loan broker, having a degree in finance or business can provide you with valuable knowledge and skills. Additionally, working in the financial industry and gaining experience in underwriting, credit analysis, and loan processing can also be beneficial.

Continue your education: The lending industry is constantly evolving, and as a loan broker, you must stay up-to-date on industry trends, regulations, and best practices. Attend industry events, read industry publications, and participate in continuing education programs to stay informed.

Build a strong network: As a loan broker, your success will depend on your ability to build relationships with clients and lenders. Attend industry events and conferences, join professional associations, and build a network of contacts that can refer clients to you.

Choose your specialty: Loan brokers can specialize in various types of loans, such as mortgage loans, commercial loans, or personal loans. Choose a specialty that aligns with your interests and expertise.

Launch your business: Once you have the necessary education, experience, licensing, and network, you can launch your loan brokerage business. Consider partnering with a mentor or coach to help you navigate the challenges of starting a new business.

Develop a strong marketing strategy: In addition to building a network, it is important to develop a marketing strategy that will help you reach potential clients. This may include creating a website, using social media, and utilizing other marketing channels that are effective in your industry.

Focus on customer service: Providing excellent customer service is essential for building a reputation as a reliable and trustworthy loan broker. Respond promptly to client inquiries, communicate clearly, and be transparent throughout the loan application and approval process.

Stay up to date with industry trends and regulations: The financial industry is constantly evolving, so it is important to stay up to date with industry trends and changes in regulations. This will help you to better understand the needs of your clients and stay ahead of the competition.

Be persistent and resilient: The loan brokerage industry can be highly competitive, so it is important to remain persistent and resilient in the face of challenges. Stay focused on your goals, be willing to learn and adapt, and always be willing to go the extra mile for your clients.

By following these tips and continuously improving your skills and knowledge, you can become a successful loan broker and build a rewarding career in the financial industry.

a. EDUCATION

Obtain the necessary education: While no formal education is required to become a loan broker, having a degree in finance, business administration, economics, or a related field can be beneficial.

While a formal education is not always required to become a loan broker, having a degree in finance, business administration, economics, or a related field can be beneficial. Here are some reasons why:

Knowledge of finance and business principles: A background in finance, business administration, or economics can provide you with a strong foundation in key concepts related to lending, financial management, and business operations.

Credibility with clients and lenders: Having a degree in a relevant field can help establish your credibility with clients and lenders. It can demonstrate your expertise and knowledge of the industry.

Understanding of legal and regulatory requirements: A degree in a relevant field can also provide an understanding of legal and regulatory requirements related to lending and finance. This can help you avoid legal issues and stay compliant with industry regulations.

Ability to analyze financial statements: As a loan broker, you will need to analyze financial statements and assess the creditworthiness of potential clients. A degree in finance or economics can help you develop the skills needed to effectively analyze financial data.

Professional development opportunities: Pursuing a degree in a relevant field can provide you with professional development and networking opportunities. You can attend industry events, join professional organizations, and connect with other professionals in the finance and lending industry.

While a degree is not always necessary to become a successful loan broker, having a strong educational background can be beneficial in many ways. It can provide you with the knowledge, skills, and credibility needed to build a successful career in this field.

b. BECOME A LOAN BROKER WITHOUT A DEGREE

In some states, loan brokers are required to have a license to operate. Requirements for licensing vary by state, but generally, you must complete a specific education program, pass a test, and meet other requirements. The shortest way to become a loan broker is to get a license.

STEP 1: Acquire the required study materials

Purchasing study materials is the initial step in becoming a loan broker. These materials are available on Amazon and at your local bookshop. These products will contain study guides, textbooks, and practice exams to aid exam preparation.

Loan broker book to pass the exams

There are several loan broker exam prep books available that can help you study for the licensing exam. Here are a few options to consider:

Loan Officer Exam Study Guide: This study guide by Loan Officer Exam can help you prepare for the loan broker licensing exam. It covers topics such as lending laws, ethical practices, and loan processing.

Mortgage Broker Examination Study Guide: This study guide by Real Estate Institute covers the topics you'll need to know for the loan broker licensing exam. It includes practice questions, quizzes, and detailed explanations of key concepts.

Loan Originator Exam Prep: This exam prep book by Mometrix Test Preparation provides a comprehensive review of loan origination concepts and practices. It includes practice tests, flashcards, and tips for passing the exam.

National Mortgage Licensing Exam Study Guide: This study guide by The Mortgage Professor covers the material you'll need to know for the loan broker licensing exam. It includes practice questions and detailed explanations of key concepts.

Loan Officer Exam Flashcard Study System: This flashcard study system by Loan Officer Exam includes hundreds of flashcards covering key concepts you'll need to know for the loan broker licensing exam.

It's important to choose a loan broker exam prep book that covers the specific topics and requirements for the licensing exam in your state. Research the different options available and read reviews to find a study guide that fits your learning style and needs.

STEP 2: Spend some days studying

Set aside few weeks to study after you acquire your study materials. To prepare for the license exam, a minimum of 20 hours of study is recommended. Focus on the essential topics and rules to pass the exam during this period.

Step three: Contemplate in-person or Online Education

While the independent study can be productive, many individuals find it beneficial to enroll in an online training course. Online training courses can provide additional help and direction as you prepare for the license exam. The National Association of Mortgage Brokers and the American Bankers Association are examples of groups that offer online training courses for loan brokers.

Organizations offering loan broker training

An essential first step in starting your loan broker business is to get the proper training. The knowledge and skills you learn during this time will be the foundation for the way you conduct your business and how it operates. You want to be sure that you do your research when selecting a commercial loan broker training program. The time and money you spend on your training will either be the best or worst investment you can make for your future professional career, so be sure you do your research when selecting the best loan broker program.

You can learn more about the Institute's commercial loan broker training options by visiting our commercial loan broker training page.

Several organizations offer loan broker training, both online and in-person. Here are a few options to consider:

National Association of Mortgage Brokers (NAMB): The NAMB offers a variety of training and education programs for loan brokers, including webinars, online courses, and in-person events. They also offer a Certified Mortgage Professional (NAMP) certification program that includes training on ethics, lending laws, and mortgage products.

LoanOfficerSchool.com: This online training provider offers courses on mortgage lending, loan processing, and other related topics. They offer both self-paced courses and live webinars, as well as in-person training at select locations.

Mortgage Training Institute: The Mortgage Training Institute offers both online and in-person training on mortgage lending and broker practices. They offer courses on topics such as mortgage fraud, compliance, and marketing for loan brokers.

American School of Business: This training provider offers in-person courses on mortgage lending, real estate, and other related topics. They offer classes in several states and offer exam prep courses for loan brokers seeking to obtain a license.

Association of Mortgage Educators (NMLS Approved Provider): This online training provider offers courses on mortgage lending, loan processing, and other related topics. They offer self-paced courses and live webinars and are approved by the National Mortgage Licensing System (NMLS).

It's important to research the specific training programs and providers to find one that best meets your needs and budget. Look for programs that are accredited, recognized by industry organizations, and offer the specific topics and training you need to be successful as a loan broker.

STEP 4: Take the licensing examination

After a weeks of preparation, it is time to take the licensure examination. In order to become a licensed loan broker, you must pass the examination. Exam subjects will include lending rules, financial statements, and credit analysis. Be sure to arrive for the exam prepared and confident, and remember to read each question slowly and thoroughly.

The organization or entity that offers a loan broker certificate test

The specific organization or entity that offers a loan broker certificate test may vary depending on your location and the type of certification you are seeking Here are some options to consider:

The National Association of Mortgage Brokers (NAMB): The NAMB offers the Certified Residential Mortgage Specialist (CRMS) certification, which is recognized by many states as a professional standard for loan brokers. To obtain this certification, you must pass an exam that tests your knowledge of mortgage lending and ethics.

The National Association of Certified Loan Officers (NACLO): The NACLO offers several certifications for loan officers and brokers, including the Certified Loan Officer (CLO) and Certified Loan Processor (CLP) designations. These certifications require passing an exam and meeting specific education and experience requirements.

The American Bankers Association (ABA): The ABA offers the Certified Lender Business Banker (CLBB) certification, which is geared towards loan officers and brokers who work with small businesses. The CLBB certification requires passing an exam and meeting specific education and experience requirements.

State licensing boards: Many states require loan brokers to obtain a license to operate. To obtain a license, you may need to pass an exam that tests your knowledge of state lending laws and regulations.

It's important to research the specific certification or licensing requirements for loan brokers in your location before choosing a certification program or exam. Make sure to choose a reputable organization or entity that is recognized in your industry and meets the requirements set by your state's licensing board.

STEP 5. Gain relevant work experience

Most loan brokers start in the lending or finance industry to gain knowledge and experience before becoming a broker.

Company that hiring commercial loan broker

Companies that hire commercial loan brokers can include:

Commercial Banks: Commercial banks often hire commercial loan brokers to help them find new clients and borrowers. Brokers can help banks identify potential borrowers and facilitate loan transactions.

Alternative Lenders: Alternative lenders such as online lenders, peer-to-peer lenders, and private equity firms may also hire commercial loan brokers to help them find new clients and borrowers. Brokers can help these lenders identify potential borrowers and connect them with financing options.

Mortgage Companies: Mortgage companies may hire commercial loan brokers to help them find clients seeking commercial mortgages. Brokers can help mortgage companies identify potential borrowers and facilitate loan transactions.

Business Services Companies: Business services companies such as accounting firms, law firms, and consulting firms may also hire commercial loan brokers to help their clients find financing options. Brokers can provide expertise and guidance to these companies' clients seeking financing.

Real Estate Brokerages: Real estate brokerages may also hire commercial loan brokers to help their clients obtain financing for commercial real estate transactions. Brokers can help real estate agents and brokers identify potential lenders and financing options for their clients.

Franchise Companies: Franchise companies may hire commercial loan brokers to help their franchisees obtain financing for opening new locations. Brokers can help franchisees identify potential lenders and financing options.

Investment Firms: Investment firms may hire commercial loan brokers to help them identify investment opportunities in the commercial lending space. Brokers can provide insight into the commercial lending market and help investment firms identify potential borrowers and lenders.

Nonprofit Organizations: Nonprofit organizations may hire commercial loan brokers to help them obtain financing for their operations or for funding specific projects. Brokers can help nonprofits identify potential lenders and financing options.

Government Agencies: Government agencies such as the Small Business Administration (SBA) may hire commercial loan brokers to help them connect small businesses with financing options. Brokers can help small businesses navigate the complex world of commercial lending and find the right financing options for their needs.

Insurance Companies: Insurance companies may hire commercial loan brokers to help their clients obtain financing for insurance-related expenses such as premiums or claims. Brokers can help insurance companies identify potential lenders and financing options for their clients.

Overall, there are many different types of companies that may hire commercial loan brokers, depending on their specific needs and interests. Brokers can provide valuable expertise and guidance to clients seeking financing in a variety of industries and contexts.

Why gaining relevant work experience

Gaining relevant work experience in the lending or finance industry is typically beneficial for aspiring loan brokers.

Here are some reasons why:

Understanding of the lending process: Working in the lending or finance industry can provide a deep understanding of the lending process, including underwriting, credit analysis, and loan documentation.

Familiarity with lenders and loan products: Working in the industry can also help you build relationships with lenders and become familiar with the various loan products available.

Experience with client interactions: Working in lending or finance can help you develop strong communication and customer service skills, essential for loan brokers who need to build relationships with clients.

Knowledge of lending laws and regulations: Working in the industry can also provide you with an understanding of lending laws and regulations, such as the Truth in Lending Act and the Fair Credit Reporting Act.

Professional network: Working in the industry can help you build a professional network of contacts, including lenders, real estate agents, and other loan brokers.

Overall, gaining work experience in the lending or finance industry can be a valuable step for aspiring loan brokers. It can provide you with the knowledge, skills, and relationships needed to succeed in this field.

Register with the National Mortgage Licensing System (NMLS): The NMLS is a nationwide database that regulates mortgage brokers and loan originators. If you plan to broker mortgage loans, you'll need to register with the NMLS and meet their requirements.

Comply with federal and state regulations: Loan brokers are subject to federal and state laws and regulations, such as the Truth in Lending Act and Fair Credit Reporting Act. Make sure to comply with all applicable regulations to avoid legal issues.

It's important to research and understands the licensing requirements for loan brokers in your state before starting your business. You may also want to consult with an attorney or business advisor to ensure that you are meeting all legal and regulatory requirements.

For people who are interested in the financial field, becoming a loan broker can be an excellent career option. Obtaining a license is the most efficient means of getting started immediately. Buy study materials, study for few weeks, take the license exam, and if you need extra support, try online training. With these steps, you may quickly obtain a loan broker license and launch your new job.

CHAPTER 3

COMMERCIAL LOAN BROKER CURRICULUM

This chapter provides an in-depth look at the curriculum of a loan broker course, highlighting the key topics covered in the training program. It offers insights into the skills, knowledge, and tools that are essential to succeed as a loan broker, covering topics such as financial analysis, commercial capital terminology, loan types and financing options, deal assessment, brokerage marketing, branding, working with clients and lenders, packaging and placement, closing deals, and staffing and business growth. Whether you are just starting out in the industry or looking to take your career to the next level, this article will give you a comprehensive overview of the curriculum and what you can expect to learn.

Introduction to Commercial Loan Brokerage

The introduction to commercial loan brokerage provides a foundational understanding of the commercial lending industry, the role of a commercial loan broker, and important legal and ethical considerations. This module sets the stage for the rest of the course by offering a broad perspective on the industry and the profession.

Overview of the commercial lending industry

The history and development of commercial lending

Key players in the industry: banks, credit unions, non-bank lenders, private lenders, and institutional investors

Market Trends and factors Affecting the commercial lending landscape

The role of government agencies and programs (e.g., Small Business Administration)

The impact of economic and financial market conditions on commercial lending

The Role of a commercial loan broker

Definition and responsibilities of a commercial loan broker

How brokers add value to the lending process for clients and lenders

The process of sourcing, negotiating, and closing commercial loans

Differences between commercial loan brokers, mortgage brokers, and direct lenders

Income and commission structures for commercial loan brokers

Skills and qualities required to be a successful commercial loan broker

Legal and ethical considerations

Licensing and regulatory requirements for commercial loan brokers

Professional Standards and Codes of Conduct

Legal and contractual obligations of commercial loan brokers to clients and lenders

Conflicts of interest and disclosure requirements

Ethical decision-making and best practices for maintaining a positive reputation in the industry

The importance of compliance with fair lending laws, privacy regulations, and anti-fraud measures

By understanding the basics of the commercial lending industry and the role of a commercial loan broker, students can better appreciate the context in which they will operate as professionals. Familiarizing oneself with legal and ethical considerations helps ensure that students are aware of their responsibilities and can navigate the industry with confidence and integrity.

Understanding Commercial Loan Types

A crucial aspect of a commercial loan broker's role is understanding the various types of commercial loans available to clients. This knowledge enables brokers to identify the most suitable financing solutions for their clients' needs. Here's an overview of the main commercial loan types:

Real estate loans

Commercial mortgage loans: Financing for purchasing or refinancing commercial properties, such as office buildings, retail centers, warehouses, or multifamily housing.

Multifamily loans: Financing specifically for the acquisition, refinancing, or rehabilitation of multifamily properties, including apartment buildings and residential complexes.

Business loans

Term loans: Fixed-term financing for businesses to fund expansion, acquisition, or other major investments.

Working capital loans: Short-term financing for businesses to cover operational expenses or temporary cash flow shortages.

Equipment financing

Equipment loans: Financing for businesses to purchase or lease machinery, vehicles, or other equipment.

Equipment leasing: Financing that allows businesses to use the equipment for a specified period without purchasing it outright.

Lines of credit

Business lines of credit: Revolving credit facilities that provide businesses with flexible access to funds for working capital, inventory management, or other operational needs.

SBA loans

U.S. Small Business Administration (SBA) guaranteed loans: Government-backed loans designed to help small businesses obtain financing with more favorable terms and lower down payments.

Construction loans

Construction financing: Short-term loans for financing the construction or renovation of commercial properties, with funds disbursed in stages based on project milestones.

Bridge loans

Short-term financing provides businesses or investors with immediate funds to cover financing or cash flow gaps, typically secured by real estate assets.

Hard money loans

Asset-based loans are provided by private investors or companies, offering fast funding and flexible underwriting but usually at higher interest rates and fees compared to traditional bank financing.

Mezzanine financing

Hybrid financing combines debt and equity elements often used for business expansion or acquisitions. Mezzanine debt is subordinate to senior debt but has priority over equity, offering lenders higher returns and potential equity participation.

By understanding the various commercial loan types, brokers can effectively assess their client's needs and offer tailored financing solutions. This knowledge also allows brokers to expand their service offerings, build relationships with diverse lenders, and increase their potential for success in the industry.

Loan Application Process

The loan application process is critical in securing commercial financing for clients. As a commercial loan broker, guiding clients through this process efficiently and effectively is critical to ensuring successful loan outcomes. Here is an overview of the main steps in the loan application process:

Pre-qualification and pre-approval

Pre-qualification: An initial assessment of a borrower's financial situation to determine their eligibility for a commercial loan. Pre-qualification provides a rough estimate of the loan amount and terms a borrower may qualify for based on factors such as credit score, income, and debt levels.

Pre-approval: A more formal evaluation of a borrower's financial situation, including a thorough review of credit reports, financial statements, and other documentation. Pre-approval results in a conditional commitment from a lender, providing the borrower with a clearer understanding of the loan amount, terms, and conditions they are likely to secure.

Gathering necessary documentation

Financial statements: Balance sheets, income statements, and cash flow statements for the business, typically for the past two to three years.

Tax returns: Personal and business tax returns for the past two to three years.

Personal financial statement: A document outlining the borrower's personal assets, liabilities, income, and expenses.

Business plan: A detailed plan outlining the purpose of the loan, the business's strategy, and projections for future growth and revenue.

Property or collateral information: Documents related to the property or collateral being used to secure the loan, such as appraisals, environmental reports, or equipment invoices.

Additional documentation: Depending on the loan type and lender requirements, other documentation may be needed, such as credit reports, legal documents, or

Loan Underwriting and Credit Analysis

Loan underwriting and credit analysis are critical steps in the commercial lending process. Lenders use this information to determine a borrower's creditworthiness and the risk of providing a loan. As a commercial loan broker, understanding these concepts will help you better assess clients' financial situations and improve your ability to secure loans for them successfully. Here are the main aspects of loan underwriting and credit analysis:

Understanding credit scores and reports

Credit scores: Numeric representations of a borrower's creditworthiness, calculated based on factors such as payment history, credit utilization, and the age of credit accounts.

Credit reports: Detailed records of a borrower's credit history, including information on loans, credit cards, payment history, and public records such as bankruptcies or liens.

Debt service coverage ratio (DSCR)

DSCR: A financial metric lenders use to assess a borrower's ability to repay a loan, calculated by dividing the borrower's net operating income by the total debt service (principal and interest payments).

A higher DSCR indicates a lower risk of default, as the borrower has more income to cover debt obligations

Loan-to-value ratio (LTV)

LTV: A ratio used by lenders to assess the risk of a loan calculated by dividing the loan amount by the appraised value of the collateral.

A lower LTV ratio indicates a lower risk for the lender, as there is a more sig equity cushion in case of default.

Analyzing financial statements

Reviewing balance sheets, income statements, and cash flow statements to assess a borrower's financial health profitability, and ability to repay a loan.

Key financial ratios, such as current ratio, quick ratio, and debt-to-equity ratio, can

Loan Packaging and Presentation

Loan packaging and presentation are crucial steps in the commercial lending process. A well-prepared and professionally presented loan package can significantly improve a borrower's chances of securing financing. As a commercial loan broker, it is essential to ensure that loan packages are complete, accurate, and effectively showcase the strengths of the borrower. Here are the main components of loan packaging and presentation:

Preparing loan proposals

Executive summary: A concise overview of the borrower's business, the purpose of the loan, and the key factors that make the borrower a good candidate for financing.

Loan request details: A clear description of the loan amount, terms, and repayment schedule being sought.

Financial analysis: A summary of the borrower's financial performance, including key financial ratios, trends, and projections.

Collateral information: A description of the collateral being offered to secure the loan, including its estimated value and any relevant documentation, such as appraisals or title reports.

Risk mitigation: A discussion of the borrower's strategies for managing and mitigating risks associated with the loan, such as contingencies for changes in market conditions or interest rates.

Loan package assembly

Organize and compile all required documentation, such as financial statements, tax returns, credit reports, property information, and legal documents, in a logical and easy-to-follow format.

Ensure that all documents are accurate, up-to-date, and complete and that any discrepancies or potential issues are addressed before submission.

Create a professional and visually appealing package with a clear table of contents, page numbering, and consistent formatting.

Presenting the loan package to lenders

Research and identify potential lenders that specialize in the type of loan being sought and have a history of working with similar borrowers.

Building Relationships with Lenders

Strong relationships with lenders are essential for commercial loan brokers to secure financing for their clients and grow their businesses. Building and maintaining a network of diverse lenders can provide brokers access to a wide range of loan products and terms, increasing the likelihood of finding suitable financing solutions for clients. Here are the key aspects of building relationships with lenders:

Identifying potential lenders

Research and create a list of lenders that offer the types of loans your clients typically require, such as banks, credit unions, non-bank lenders, private lenders, and institutional investors.

Consider working with local and national lenders, as each may have unique advantages and preferences.

Attend industry events, conferences, and networking functions to meet new lenders and stay informed about trends in the lending market.

Establishing and maintaining lender relationships

Introduce yourself and your brokerage to potential lenders, highlighting your experience, expertise, and the value you can bring to their business.

Keep communication channels open and maintain regular contact with lenders, updating them on your client's needs and any changes in your business or the market.

Demonstrate professionalism and reliability by providing accurate and complete loan packages, promptly addressing any lender concerns or requests for additional information, and following through on commitments.

Show appreciation for successful loan transactions by thanking lenders and acknowledging their efforts.

Communication and negotiation strategies

Be clear, concise, and honest in all communications with lenders, avoiding jargon and ensuring that all parties understand the terms and conditions of the loan.

Listen carefully to lenders' concerns and preferences, and be prepared to negotiate on behalf of your clients to secure the best possible loan terms.

Maintain a positive and respectful attitude during negotiations, focusing on problem-solving and finding mutually beneficial solutions.

Understanding lender preferences and requirements

Familiarize yourself with each lender's unique loan products, underwriting guidelines, and documentation requirements.

Learn about lenders' preferences regarding loan types, industries, geographic regions, and borrower profiles.

Keep up-to-date with any changes in lender policies or requirements, and adjust your loan packaging and submission process accordingly.

By building strong relationships with lenders, commercial loan brokers can increase their chances of securing financing for clients and develop a reputation as reliable and effective partners in the commercial lending industry.

Marketing and Building Your Loan Brokerage Business

Effective marketing is crucial for the growth and success of your commercial loan brokerage business. By implementing a well-rounded marketing strategy, you can attract new clients, increase brand awareness, and establish a strong reputation in the industry. Here are the key aspects of marketing and building your loan brokerage business:

Defining your target market

Identify the types of clients you want to serve, such as small business owners, commercial property investors, or specific industries.

Analyze your target market's demographics, needs, and preferences to tailor your marketing messages and offerings.

Branding and positioning

Develop a unique brand identity that reflects your brokerage's values, expertise, and the benefits you provide to clients.

Position your brokerage as a reliable and trustworthy partner in the commercial lending industry, focusing on your experience, knowledge, and commitment to client success.

Developing a marketing plan

Set clear marketing objectives, such as increasing brand awareness, generating leads, or building client relationships.

Outline the strategies and tactics you will use to achieve your objectives, including online and offline marketing channels, networking, and referrals.

Allocate a budget for your marketing activities and regularly track and measure the effectiveness of your efforts.

Online and offline marketing strategies

Online marketing: Utilize digital channels such as your website, email marketing, search engine optimization (SEO), and pay-per-click (PPC) advertising to reach potential clients and drive traffic to your website.

Offline marketing: Leverage traditional marketing methods such as print advertising, direct mail, and event sponsorships to increase brand visibility and engage with your target audience.

Networking and referrals

Attend industry events, conferences, and networking functions to meet potential clients, lenders, and other professionals in the commercial lending industry.

Build

Client Management and Customer Service

Effective client management and customer service are essential for building strong relationships with clients, ensuring their satisfaction, and securing repeat business and referrals. By focusing on delivering exceptional service throughout the commercial lending process, commercial loan brokers can differentiate themselves from competitors and foster long-lasting client relationships. Here are the key aspects of client management and customer service:

Building rapport with clients

Take the time to understand each client's unique needs, preferences, and goals, demonstrating genuine interest in their success.

Be approachable, friendly, and professional in all interactions, creating a comfortable environment for clients to ask questions and share concerns.

Maintain open and transparent communication, providing clients with regular updates on their loan application progress and promptly addressing any concerns.

Managing client expectations

Clearly explain the commercial lending process, including potential challenges and timeframes, to set realistic expectations.

Be honest about the likelihood of securing financing and the potential terms and conditions, avoiding overpromising or providing misleading information. Continuously update clients on any changes or developments affecting their loan applications, managing their expectations throughout the process.

Communication and follow-up strategies

Establish a consistent communication schedule with clients, using their preferred method of communication (e.g., phone, email, or in-person meetings).

Promptly respond to client inquiries and requests for information, demonstrating your commitment to their needs and concerns.

Follow up with clients after the loan process to gather feedback, address any post-closing issues, and maintain the relationship for potential future business or referrals.

Resolving issues and handling objections

Actively listen to client concerns and objections, acknowledging their feelings and demonstrating empathy.

Provide clear and concise explanations or solutions, addressing the root cause of the issue and offering alternatives when necessary.

Remain calm and professional during difficult conversations, focusing on finding mutually beneficial resolutions and maintaining client trust.

Closing the deal and post-closing services

Guide clients through the final stages of the loan process, including signing loan documents and coordinating with lenders and other involved parties to ensure a smooth closing.

Celebrate the successful completion of the loan with clients, expressing gratitude for their business and reinforcing the positive aspects of the experience.

Offer post-closing services, such as ongoing loan management, financial consulting, or assistance with future financing needs, to solidify your relationship with clients and encourage long-term loyalty.

By focusing on exceptional client management and customer service, commercial loan brokers can build strong client relationships, improve client satisfaction, and ultimately grow their businesses through repeat business and referrals.

Compliance and Regulation

Complying with relevant laws and regulations is essential for commercial loan brokers to operate legally, protect their clients, and maintain a strong reputation in the industry. By staying informed about the latest regulatory requirements and implementing appropriate compliance measures, brokers can minimize legal risks and ensure the long-term success of their businesses. Here are the key aspects of compliance and regulation in the commercial loan brokerage industry:

Licensing Requirements for commercial loan brokers

Licensing requirements for commercial loan brokers vary by state and may include completing a licensing application, passing a background check, completing pre-licensing education, and passing a licensing exam.

Some states may also require brokers to maintain a surety bond, which provides financial protection for clients in the event of misconduct or failure to comply with licensing requirements.

Check with your state's licensing agency or Department of financial services to determine the specific requirements for your area.

State and federal regulations

Commercial loan brokers must adhere to state and federal regulations governing the lending industry, such as the Truth in Lending Act (TILA), the Real Estate Settlement Procedures Act (RESPA), and the Dodd-Frank Wall Street Reform and Consumer Protection Act.

Stay informed about regulatory changes at the state and federal levels and ensure that your brokerage's policies and procedures are updated accordingly.

Privacy and data protection laws

Be aware of privacy and data protection laws, such as the Health Insurance Portability and Accountability Act (HIPAA) or the California Consumer Privacy Act (CCPA) which regulate the collection, use, storage, and disclosure of clients' personal information.

Implement appropriate data security measures, such as encryption and secure storage, to protect clients' sensitive information and maintain privacy.

Anti-money laundering and fraud prevention

Comply with the Bank Secrecy

Technology and Tools for Loan Brokers

Leveraging technology and tools can help commercial loan brokers streamline their operations, improve efficiency, and enhance the overall client experience. By adopting the right solutions for your brokerage, you can optimize various aspects of your business, from client management to financial analysis. Here are some key technology and tools for loan brokers:

Loan origination software

Loan origination software simplifies the loan application and underwriting process by automating tasks, such as document collection, data verification, and credit analysis.

These systems can help brokers save time, reduce errors, and improve the overall efficiency of the lending process.

Customer relationship management (CRM) systems

CRM systems help brokers manage client relationships by organizing and tracking client information, communications, and interactions.

These tools can help you stay organized, maintain consistent communication with clients, and monitor the progress of loan applications throughout the lending process.

Financial analysis tools

Financial analysis tools, such as Excel or specialized software, can help brokers analyze clients' financial statements, calculate key financial ratios, and assess creditworthiness.

These tools can save time and improve the accuracy of your financial assessments, allowing you to better advice clients and negotiate with lenders.

Document management and e-signature solutions

Document management systems help brokers store, organize, and access client documents, ensuring that information is secure, easy to find, and up to date.

E-signature solutions, such as DocuSign or Adobe Sign, enable clients to sign loan documents electronically, streamlining the loan closing process and reducing the need for physical paperwork.

Online marketing and social media tools

Online marketing tools, such as email marketing platforms, SEO software, and social media management systems, can help brokers create and manage digital marketing campaigns to attract new clients and increase brand awareness.

Social media tools like Hootsuite or Buffer allow you to schedule and manage your social media posts across multiple platforms, helping you maintain a consistent online presence and engage with your target audience.

By incorporating the right technology and tools into your commercial loan brokerage business, you can improve efficiency, enhance the client experience, and ultimately achieve greater success in the industry.

Continuing Education and Professional Development

Continuing education and professional development are crucial for commercial loan brokers to stay competitive, enhance their skills, and adapt to changes in the industry. By actively pursuing learning opportunities and staying informed about the latest trends and best practices, brokers can provide better service to their clients and grow their businesses. Here are some key aspects of continuing education and professional development for loan brokers:

Staying updated on industry trends and changes

Regularly read industry publications, newsletters, and blogs to stay informed about new developments, market trends, and regulatory changes in the commercial lending industry.

Monitor economic indicators, such as interest rates, real estate market trends, and business growth patterns, to anticipate potential changes that could affect your clients and your business.

Networking and joining professional associations

Join professional associations, such as the National Association of Mortgage Brokers (NAMB) or the Mortgage Bankers Association (MBA), to connect with industry peers, share knowledge, and gain access to valuable resources.

Participate in local networking events, such as the chamber of commerce meetings or real estate investment groups, to meet potential clients, partners, and referral sources.

Attending workshops, seminars, and conferences

Attend industry workshops, seminars, and conferences to learn about new techniques, technologies, and best practices in the commercial lending industry.

Participate in training sessions and educational events offered by lenders, vendors, and other industry partners to deepen your understanding of specific loan products and processes.

CHAPTER 4

SOME LOAN BROKER EXAM QUESTIONS AND ANSWER

1. What is a commercial loan broker?

A commercial loan broker is a financial professional who works as a middleman between borrowers and lenders. Their job is to help business owners secure financing by connecting them with appropriate lenders and assisting them in navigating the loan application process.

2. What are the key responsibilities of a commercial loan broker?

The key responsibilities of a commercial loan broker include identifying potential lenders, evaluating loan applications, negotiating loan terms, and ensuring compliance with applicable regulations. They may also assist borrowers with preparing loan documentation and providing financial advice.

3. What qualifications are required to become a commercial loan broker?

In most cases, a commercial loan broker must have a bachelor's degree in finance, business administration, or a related field. They should also have experience in the financial industry and possess strong communication and negotiation skills. Many states require commercial loan brokers to obtain a license, which typically involves passing an exam and meeting certain education and experience requirements.

4. What are the main types of commercial loans?

The main types of commercial loans include term loans, lines of credit, SBA loans, and commercial real estate loans. Each type of loan has its own unique features and requirements, and it is up to the commercial loan broker to identify the best financing option for their client.

5. What factors should a commercial loan broker consider when evaluating a loan application?

When evaluating a loan application, a commercial loan broker should consider factors such as the borrower's credit history, financial statements, collateral, and business plan. They should also consider the lender's requirements and underwriting criteria to ensure that the borrower is a good fit for the loan program.

6. **What are the typical fees associated with commercial loan brokers?**

Commercial loan brokers typically charge a commission based on the loan amount, which can range from 1% to 5% or more. They may also charge application fees or other upfront costs.

7. **What are the advantages of using a commercial loan broker?**

Using a commercial loan broker can save time and effort by simplifying the loan application process, providing access to a broader range of lenders, and helping borrowers secure better loan terms.

8. **What are the disadvantages of using a commercial loan broker?**

The main disadvantage of using a commercial loan broker is the cost, as they typically charge fees that can add up to thousands of dollars. Additionally, brokers may have conflicts of interest if they are incentivized to steer borrowers toward certain lenders.

9. **How can commercial loan brokers stay up-to-date with industry trends and regulations?**

Commercial loan brokers can stay up-to-date by attending industry conferences, reading industry publications, and participating in professional organizations. They may also need to complete continuing education courses to maintain their license.

10. **What are the key skills required to be a successful commercial loan broker?**

Successful commercial loan brokers should have strong communication skills, negotiation skills, and financial analysis skills. They should also be able to build relationships with lenders and borrowers and have a strong understanding of lending regulations and industry trends.

11. **What are some common mistakes that commercial loan brokers should avoid?**

Common mistakes that commercial loan brokers should avoid include failing to vet borrowers properly, failing to disclose all fees and costs upfront, and steering borrowers toward loans that are not in their best interest.

12. **How can commercial loan brokers help borrowers improve their chances of securing a loan?**

Commercial loan brokers can help borrowers improve their chances of securing a loan by assisting with loan preparation, providing guidance on credit and financial statements, and identifying lenders that are a good fit for the borrower's needs.

13. How do commercial loan brokers evaluate the creditworthiness of a borrower?

Commercial loan brokers typically evaluate a borrower's creditworthiness by reviewing their credit history, financial statements, and business plan. They may also consider the borrower's collateral and industry experience.

14. What is the difference between a mortgage broker and a commercial loan broker?

While both mortgage brokers and commercial loan brokers work as intermediaries between borrowers and lenders, mortgage brokers focus specifically on residential mortgages, while commercial loan brokers specialize in commercial loans.

15. What are some common misconceptions about commercial loan brokers?

Common misconceptions about commercial loan brokers include that they can guarantee loan approval, that they are the only way to access commercial financing, and that their fees are always high. In reality, loan approval is never guaranteed, there are many ways to access commercial financing, and brokers' fees can vary widely.

16. **How do commercial loan brokers help lenders?**

Commercial loan brokers can help lenders by providing them with a stream of qualified loan applicants, assisting with underwriting and due diligence, and ensuring compliance with applicable regulations.

17. **What are the most common types of lenders that commercial loan brokers work with?**

Commercial loan brokers work with a wide range of lenders, including banks, credit unions, private lenders, and government agencies such as the Small Business Administration (SBA).

18. **What is the difference between recourse and non-recourse loans?**

Recourse loans are loans where the borrower is personally liable for repaying the loan, while non-recourse loans are loans where the lender can only look to the collateral for repayment.

19. **What are some common types of collateral for commercial loans?**

Common types of collateral for commercial loans include real estate, equipment, inventory, accounts receivable, and intellectual property.

20. **How do commercial loan brokers help borrowers find the best loan terms?**

Commercial loan brokers can help borrowers find the best loan terms by negotiating with lenders on their behalf, comparing loan offers, and providing guidance on which loan programs are the best fit for their needs.

21. **What are some of the most important factors that lenders consider when evaluating a loan application?**

Lenders consider a variety of factors when evaluating a loan application, including the borrower's credit history, cash flow, collateral, and industry experience.

22. **How do commercial loan brokers ensure that loan applications are complete and accurate?**

Commercial loan brokers typically work closely with borrowers to gather all necessary documentation, review the application for completeness and accuracy, and follow up with lenders as needed to ensure that the loan process goes smoothly.

23. **What are some common loan documents that borrowers are required to provide?**

Common loan documents that borrowers are required to provide include financial statements, tax returns, business plans, and personal guarantees.

24. **How do commercial loan brokers stay objective and avoid conflicts of interest?**

Commercial loan brokers should always act in the best interests of their clients and avoid any conflicts of interest. They may disclose any potential conflicts upfront and ensure that they are transparent about their fees and compensation.

25. **What are some common reasons why loan applications are rejected?**

Loan applications may be rejected for a variety of reasons, including poor credit history, insufficient collateral, lack of cash flow, and incomplete or inaccurate documentation.

26. How do commercial loan brokers market their services to potential borrowers?

Commercial loan brokers may market their services through online advertising, networking events, referrals from satisfied clients, and partnerships with other professionals such as accountants or attorneys.

27. What are some common loan programs offered by the Small Business Administration (SBA)?

The Small Business Administration (SBA) offers a variety of loan programs for small businesses, including the 7(a) loan program, the Microloan program, and the CDC/504 loan program.

28. What is a bridge loan, and how is it used in commercial lending?

A bridge loan is a short-term loan that is used to bridge a financing gap between the purchase of a property and the long-term financing. It is often used in commercial real estate lending.

29. What is the difference between a fixed-rate and variable-rate loan?

A fixed-rate loan has a fixed interest rate for the life of the loan, while a variable-rate loan has an interest rate that can fluctuate over time based on market conditions.

30. **What are some common loan covenants that borrowers may be required to agree to?**

Common loan covenants include requirements for maintaining a certain level of financial performance, restrictions on taking on additional debt, and limitations on certain types of business activities.

31. **What is the loan-to-value (LTV) ratio, and how is it used in commercial lending?**

The loan-to-value (LTV) ratio is the ratio of the loan amount to the appraised value of the collateral. It is used by lenders to determine the risk of the loan and to set the loan terms.

32. **What is a personal guarantee, and when is it required in commercial lending?**

A personal guarantee is a promise by an individual to personally repay a loan if the business is unable to do so. It is often required in commercial lending if the borrower has a limited track record or insufficient collateral.

33. **How do commercial loan brokers help borrowers navigate the loan application process?**

Commercial loan brokers can help borrowers navigate the loan application process by providing guidance on what documentation is required, helping to prepare loan packages, and advocating on behalf of the borrower with lenders.

34. **What is a balloon payment, and how is it used in commercial lending?**

A balloon payment is a large, one-time payment that is due at the end of a loan term. It is often used in commercial lending as a way to reduce monthly payments or to provide flexibility in the repayment schedule.

35. **How do commercial loan brokers ensure that borrowers are aware of all costs and fees associated with a loan?**

Commercial loan brokers should always be transparent about the costs and fees associated with a loan, and should provide borrowers with a detailed breakdown of all expenses. They may also provide guidance on how to minimize fees and costs wherever possible.

36. **What is debt service coverage ratio, and how is it used in commercial lending?**

The debt service coverage ratio (DSCR) is a measure of a borrower's ability to service debt payments. It is calculated by dividing the borrower's net operating income by their debt service obligations. Lenders use the DSCR to evaluate the risk of a loan and to set loan terms.

37. **What is the difference between a term loan and a line of credit?**

A term loan is a loan with a fixed repayment schedule and a set term, while a line of credit is a revolving loan that can be drawn upon as needed up to a predetermined credit limit.

38. **What is a mezzanine loan, and how is it used in commercial lending?**

A mezzanine loan is a type of financing that sits between senior debt and equity in the capital structure. It is often used to fund growth or acquisitions, and typically has higher interest rates and more flexible repayment terms than traditional debt.

39. What is a prepayment penalty, and when is it applied in commercial lending?

A prepayment penalty is a fee that is charged to borrowers who pay off a loan before the end of its term. It is applied in commercial lending to compensate lenders for the loss of interest income.

40. What is an interest-only loan, and how is it used in commercial lending?

An interest-only loan is a loan where the borrower only pays interest on the principal for a set period of time. It is often used in commercial lending as a way to reduce initial payments or to provide flexibility in the repayment schedule.

41. How do commercial loan brokers evaluate the potential risks associated with a loan application?

Commercial loan brokers evaluate the potential risks associated with a loan application by conducting due diligence on the borrower, analyzing their credit history and financial statements, and evaluating the collateral that will be used to secure the loan.

42. **What is the role of underwriting in commercial lending, and how do commercial loan brokers assist with the underwriting process?**

Underwriting is the process of evaluating the risk of a loan and determining the appropriate loan terms. Commercial loan brokers assist with the underwriting process by preparing loan packages, providing guidance on borrower qualifications and creditworthiness, and advocating on behalf of the borrower with lenders.

43. **What are some common types of commercial real estate loans?**

Common types of commercial real estate loans include bridge loans, construction loans, permanent loans, and SBA 504 loans.

44. **What is the difference between recourse and non-recourse loans in commercial real estate lending?**

Recourse loans in commercial real estate lending allow the lender to pursue legal action against the borrower personally if they default on the loan, while non-recourse loans limit the lender's recourse to the collateral securing the loan.

45. **What are some common types of lenders that offer commercial real estate loans?**

Common types of lenders that offer commercial real estate loans include banks, credit unions, private lenders, and real estate investment trusts (REITs).

CHAPTER 6

SETTING UP A LOAN BROKER JOB AS BUSINESS

CONDUCTING FIELD RESEARCH FOR THE LOAN BROKER BUSINESS

Before starting your loan broker business, it is important to consider various factors, including market research and business structure. In the United States, there are various business structures to choose from, such as sole proprietorships, partnerships, limited liability partnerships, and corporations, each with its own paperwork, taxes, fees, and restrictions. It is important to understand how each structure affects taxes, operations, and personal assets.

Conducting field research

Conducting field research is also crucial to the success of your commercial loan broker business. This involves gaining familiarity with the market and conducting a thorough analysis of the industry, including demographics, customer behavior, financial capacity, and potential competitors. It is important to estimate the necessary capital and operating expenses to ensure the business can thrive.

Market and competitor research

Market and competitor research is also crucial, as i allows you to determine what sets your business apar and identify opportunities to improve your product o service. This can be done through primary research such as surveys and interviews with potential customers and secondary research, utilizing existing data source like census data.

A SWOT analysis

A SWOT analysis can help identify the strengths weaknesses, opportunities, and threats of your busines idea, allowing you to make informed decisions about it viability and potential for success. Considering thes factors before starting your commercial loan broke business, you can position yourself for success in th competitive US market.

Create your business plan.

- The executive summary should appear first in th business plan, but it should be written last. defines the proposed new business and highlight the company's goals and strategies fc accomplishing them.
- Company Description: This section highlights th problems that your product or service solves an why your business or concept is superior. Fc

example, if you have a background in molecular engineering and have used that knowledge to design a new sort of sports clothing, you have the essential qualifications to manufacture the greatest material.

- Market analysis: This component of the business plan assesses how well-positioned a firm is relative to its competitors. Included in the market study should be the target market, segmentation analysis, market size, growth rate, trends, and assessment of the competitive landscape.

- Organization and structure: Describe the anticipated corporate structure, the proposed risk management measures, and the management people. What are their qualifications? Will your firm be a single-member limited liability company (LLC) or a corporation?

- Mission and objectives: This part should include a brief mission statement as well as a summary of the organization's goals and strategies for accomplishing them. These goals should be SMART (specific, measurable, action-orientated, realistic, and time-bound).

- Products or services: This part defines your company's operations. It contains the items you will offer customers at the commencement of your firm, how they compare to your rivals, how much they will cost, who will be responsible for generating them, how you will acquire resources, and how much they will cost to construct.

- The most time-consuming element of a business plan to prepare is the background summary. Compile and summarize any data, articles, and research papers on trends that might have a good or negative impact on your firm or sector.

- Marketing strategy: The marketing plan describes the characteristics of your product or service, summarizes the SWOT analysis, and evaluates the competition. Additionally, it explains how your firm will be advertised, how much will be spent on marketing, and how long the campaign is expected to run.

- Financial plan: The financial plan is perhaps the most crucial component of the business plan, as the firm cannot develop without funds. Include in your financial plan a planned budget and anticipated financial statements, including an income statement, a balance sheet, and a statement of cash flows. Generally, financial estimates for five years are reasonable. You should also put your financing proposal in this area if you are seeking external support.

Nota bene: if you cannot design a business plan, they are experts who can accomplish everything for you if you offer them your ideas. I recommend that you contact www.fiverr.com for assistance. On FIVERR, you can get a professional business plan for less than $300.

Plan your exit strategy.

have an exit strategy that details how to be prepared for how the firm will be sold or ownership transferred if the owner decides to retire or move on to other initiatives. Additionally, an exit strategy enables you to maximize the value of your business when it comes time to sell. There are several methods for leaving a firm, and the greatest one for you will rely on your objectives and circumstances.

These are the most prevalent exit strategies:
- Selling the company to a third party
- Transferring it to family members

- Selling the company's assets; and
- Closing the doors and leaving.

LEGAL MATTER: LAWFULLY CREATE YOUR BUSINESS.

Step 1: Choose a structure for your commercial loan broker business.

Because most states require businesses, including LLCs, corporations, and partnerships, to register with state authorities if they conduct business in the state, I propose forming an LLC for this Laundromat Business. In addition, the legal position of an LLC helps you to avoid liability if something negative occurs to the business. If you own a business, your state requires you to register it.

- physical presence inside the state
- Throughout-person meetings with clients in the state.
- Receiving a substantial share of the company's income from the state.

- Employment is an example of business operations in the state.

Why choose an LLC as a structure?

An LLC minimizes your personal accountability for business obligations. One or more persons or corporations can own LLCs, and they are required to have a registered agent. These proprietors are called members.

- LLCs give liability protection to their owners
- They are one of the easiest corporate formations to form
- A single-member LLC is possible
- You may be needed to complete extra documents on a regular basis with your state.
- LLCs are not authorized to issue shares, and yearly filing costs must be paid to the state.
- The vending machine company must thus be registered with the state.
- In most circumstances, you may register your business through the secretary of state's office, but you should verify your state's regulations first.

To register your business in a state, you must choose a registered agent to accept official paperwork and correspondence on your behalf. The registered agent must reside in the same state as the registered office of the firm.

Step 2: Choose a Company Name.

The business name is the legal name that will identify your Laundromat Business. To receive an EIN, you must submit a completed Form SS-4 with your business name. To register a business name, you must first create the relevant formation documents, such as an LLC operating agreement, and file them with the appropriate state office. To be registered, the business name must be accessible in the state of the establishment. Check with the state department to see whether the name is still available. In most states, the Company Division of the Secretary of State provides a business name lookup tool.

DBA vs. Business Name.

DBA stands for "Doing Business As" and refers to false business names. If your company operates under a name different than its legal name, you may be required to register a DBA. "Mike's Bike Shop" is sometimes referred to as "Mike's Bikes." Mike's Bike Shop is the company's legal name, while "Mike's Bikes" is its DBA.

The offices of your state, county, or municipality may demand a DBA. A DBA can be used to register a business bank account, as a "trade name" to market your products and services, and to get a business license.

Step 3: Register Your Business.

To formally establish a corporation, LLC, or other business organization, forms must be submitted to the state's business department, often the Secretary of State. You must choose a registered agent to accept legal papers on your behalf as part of this procedure. Additionally, you must pay a filing fee. The state will provide you a certificate that may be used to apply for licenses, a Taxpayer Identification Number (TIN), and company bank accounts.

Step 4: Get an Employer Identification Number or Tax Identification Number

Businesses are issued a nine-digit federal tax identification number (commonly known as an Employer Identification Number or EIN). However, sole owners and single-member LLCs with no workers may be permitted to utilize the owner's Social Security number as an alternative. You may receive an EIN for free via the IRS website, which gives precise, extensive information regarding requirements on its EIN application page.

Except for sole proprietorships with no workers, all firms are required to get an EIN. You should receive your EIN within minutes after submitting your application to the IRS (**https://www.irs.gov/businesses/small-businesses-se lf-employed/how-to-apply-for-an-ein**).

Step 5: Open a business bank account

Separation of personal and business finances: By opening a separate commercial business account, you can keep your personal and business finances separate. This helps you to better manage your finances and makes it easier to track expenses, income, and cash flow.

Professionalism: Having a commercial business account shows that you are serious about your business and helps to establish your credibility with clients, suppliers, and other stakeholders. It also makes it easier to handle transactions, including receiving payments and paying bills.

Access to financing: Opening a commercial business account is often a requirement when applying for loans or other forms of financing. Lenders typically require businesses to have a separate commercial account to help them assess the financial health of the business and determine its eligibility for financing.

Protection of personal assets: Separating personal and business finances helps to protect personal assets in case of legal action or bankruptcy. By having a separate commercial business account, creditors are less likely to go after personal assets in the event that the business is unable to pay its debts.

Overall, opening a commercial business account is an important step for any business owner looking to establish and grow their business. It helps to keep finances organized, demonstrates professionalism, and provides access to financing opportunities while protecting personal assets.

Step 6 : Permissions & Licensing

The licensing requirements for starting a loan broker business vary by state and may depend on the types of loans you plan to broker. Here are some general requirements to keep in mind. Although the majority of states do not require a broker to be licensed in order to start a loan broker firm, some do. For those who do, the obligation is often confined to mortgages. The easiest approach to learning whether or not a license is required in your state is to conduct research. There is a licensing board in each state that can offer this information. You may also contact member organizations within the banking industry or your local Small Business Administration office. **https://www.sba.gov/**:

Obtain a business license: You may need to obtain a general business license from your state or local government before starting your loan brokerage business.

Renew your license: Most loan broker licenses need to be renewed periodically, typically every year or two. Stay up-to-date with your state's renewal requirements to maintain your license.

It's important to note that the licensing requirements for loan brokers may be different depending on the types of loans you plan to broker. For example, if you plan to broker mortgage loans, you may need to meet additional requirements through the National Mortgage Licensing System (NMLS).

Step 7: Commercial Insurance.

Liability concerns can never be removed, regardless of how well an organization is managed. Risk is an inevitable aspect of conducting business, and it pays to be prepared for it. Depending on the circumstances, certain insurance plans, such as vehicle insurance, may be mandated by law as a precaution. Numerous organizations rely on an insurance broker to assist them in determining the optimal "coverages" (and levels of coverage) for their purposes, such as the following types:

- General liability insurance is the very minimum need for any firm. It covers against virtually all business-related risks, such as property damage and personal injury.

- Product liability insurance protects against alleged injuries caused by defective products and may be required for firms that make and sell any type of product.

- Professional liability insurance, commonly known as "errors and omissions insurance," protects employees against allegations of professional negligence.

- Commercial property insurance provides additional protection for land and buildings that might be destroyed by fire, water, or vandalism.

- In all states except Texas, workers' compensation insurance covers employees who are injured on the job.

Auto liability insurance covers accidents involving business-owned automobiles and personnel driving on company time.

Prepare for Taxes

Tax preparation is one of the most critical factors when launching a laundromat business. Taxes may be difficult, and you may be required to pay income tax, self-employment tax, sales tax, and property tax, among others, depending on how you prioritize your Laundromat Business. Consider hiring an accountant if you can't manage it. The pricing on www.Fiverr.com is substantially cheaper.

Checklist

- Determine the right business structure for your needs.

- Determine the jurisdiction where you wish to incorporate your LLC (Limited Liability Company).

How to become a commercial loan broker without a degree.

- Find a registered agent in your region.

- If applicable, register your LLC or S-corporation.

- Obtain an EIN (Employer Identification Number).

- Obtain an address in the United States if required.

- Establish a bank account in the U.S.

- Establish a merchant account in order to accept consumer payments.

- Obtain commercial insurance.

- Obtain a local United States telephone number for your new business.

- Determine your expected tax liability.

- Ensure that your personal and corporate accounts remain separate.

- Pay any yearly fees as well as any other applicable payments.

- Ensure compliance with all applicable local, county, state, and federal requirements.

CONCLUSION

This book has provided you with a comprehensive roadmap to launching and growing a successful commercial loan brokerage business. By following the steps outlined in this book, you can overcome the absence of a formal degree and still achieve a thriving career in the industry.

From understanding the fundamentals of commercial lending and building relationships with lenders to mastering the loan application process and leveraging technology for greater efficiency, this guide has equipped you with the knowledge and tools necessary to navigate the complex world of commercial lending. Additionally, the importance of marketing, client management, and compliance has been emphasized, ensuring that you can build a solid foundation for your business and foster long-lasting relationships with clients and lenders alike.

Finally, this guide has highlighted the value of ongoing education and professional development, demonstrating that learning should never stop – even after you have established your business. By staying informed, adapting to changes in the industry, and continually honing your skills, you can maintain your competitive edge and achieve lasting success as a commercial loan broker without a degree.

Remember, the path to success in the commercial loan brokerage industry may be challenging, but with dedication, hard work, and a commitment to excellence, you can overcome any obstacles and build a fulfilling and profitable career. Now that you have the knowledge and tools at your disposal, it's time to take the first step on your journey to becoming a successful commercial loan broker. Good luck, and may your new venture be prosperous and rewarding!

BIBLIOGRAPHY

Berg, G. (2016). The Complete Guide to Financing Real Estate Developments. New York: AMACOM.

Best, G. (2020). The Loan Officer's Practical Guide to Residential Finance. San Diego, CA: QuickStart Publications.

Chodorow, A. (2014). The Entrepreneur's Guide to Financial Statements. Santa Barbara, CA: Praeger.

Colley, J. (2017). The Art of Commercial Lending. CreateSpace Independent Publishing Platform.

Cummings, C. (2015). The Little Black Book of Commercial Lending. CreateSpace Independent Publishing Platform.

Fisher, J. (2019). The Commercial Real Estate Investor's Handbook: A Step-by-Step Roadmap to Financial Wealth. New York: BiggerPockets Publishing.

Geller, D. (2018). Financial Statement Analysis: The Blueprint for Investing Success. New York: Wiley.

Halloran, M. (2016). The Handbook of Loan Syndications and Trading. New York: McGraw-Hill Education.

Leicht, K. & Fitzgerald, S. (2021). Mastering the Art of Commercial Real Estate Investing. New York: Morgan James Publishing.

Pozin, G. (2019). The Startup's Guide to Building a Winning Sales Strategy. CreateSpace Independent Publishing Platform.

Thomas, A. (2018). The Ultimate Sales Machine Turbocharge Your Business with Relentless Focus on 12 Key Strategies. New York: Penguin Books.

Tracy, B. (2015). The Psychology of Selling: Increase Your Sales Faster and Easier Than You Ever Thought Possible. New York: HarperCollins.

ABOUT THE AUTHOR

Fred Faithson is an accomplished professional with a diverse background in public administration (MPA) and History of International Relations. With a passion for helping others succeed, Fred has combined his expertise in these fields with his passion for entrepreneurship to create a comprehensive guide for aspiring commercial loan brokers.

Drawing on his extensive knowledge and real-world experience, Fred has crafted a step-by-step guide that empowers individuals without a formal degree to enter and excel in the commercial lending industry. By breaking down complex concepts into easily digestible sections, Fred's work demystifies the world of commercial lending and provides practical advice for success in the field.

Made in the USA
Las Vegas, NV
01 May 2024

89400002R00066